Anxiety

Comprehensive Handbook For Liberating Oneself From Excessive Rumination And Attaining Serenity Through Pragmatic Strategies

(What Is Anxiety And Effective Strategies For Mitigating Anxiety)

Ted Livingston

TABLE OF CONTENT

Taming The Anxious Brain 1

Approaches To Achieving Mastery In Any Field 6

Methods For Engaging In Guided Imagery Techniques 13

Engaging In The Application Of Cognitive Behavioral Therapy. 30

How To Handle Fear 47

How To Transition From Avoiding Individuals To Embracing Their Participation In Our Personal Development 51

Enhancing Sociability In The Professional Environment 63

Understanding Anxiety Disorder 71

Group Therapy And The Application Of Act 77

Relaxation Techniques 89

Effective Strategies For Anxiety And Panic Management 110

The Significance Of Couple Stability And The Motivations Behind Its Pursuit...................... 130

Taming The Anxious Brain

Are you aware that anxiety can be classified as a type of arousal? Indeed, it can be discerned as a manifestation of arousal, whereby various physiological responses akin to those experienced during sexual arousal are initiated. The heart rate accelerates, perspiration may ensue, and, ultimately, rapid thoughts commence. The circulation of blood is accelerated, leading to cognitive impairment for individuals who find themselves in such a heightened state. Rapidly racing thoughts serve as a prominent element of anxiety, as they engender a state where the mind engages in swift cognition, thereby diverting attention and neglecting various other tasks. It will not endeavor to allocate sufficient time for the deliberation of the decisions you undertake. The attention will, nevertheless, be directed towards impulsivity. If I were required to deliver a public address (a daunting task often considered more fearful than death itself, which is why it is frequently employed as an exemplar), and if I am feeling apprehensive, it implies that I will lack the mental composure necessary to adequately evaluate the circumstances. Indeed, while I have diligently crafted an eloquent discourse, the mounting apprehension would hinder my ability to present the speech as envisioned. There is a higher probability that I would commit an error. In this instance, the presence of anxiety is contributing to a scenario where the desired outcome becomes increasingly susceptible to manifestation. Therefore, the objective of this chapter is to assist individuals in effectively moderating their cognitive processes amidst the onset of anxiety. It is inconsequential whether it is a matter as elementary as deliberate counting and deep inhalation. You may avail yourself of tranquil images that you can engage with to decelerate those ruminations. Perhaps you could consider engaging in a suitable physical activity that would enable your cognitive processes to transition away from the fight or flight response, as this is precisely the physiological reaction experienced by many individuals when anxiety arises. The purpose of a racing mind is to enable you to arrive at a prompt and apparent decision in a given situation, yet it should be noted that this does not necessarily guarantee the optimal decision. The state of racing thoughts hampers an individual's ability to apply their acquired decision-making skills, rendering them akin to a disoriented fish thrashing about aimlessly. Consider a highly active mind as a large vessel navigating turbulent waters without any mooring, aimlessly meandering. By employing correct breathing techniques, you can effectively calm your mind and alleviate the source of your anxiety. It takes practice though. Were you aware that at this particular moment, should you choose to close your eyes and contemplate a specific situation that elicits anxiety for you, it is likely that you will begin to experience feelings of anxiety? When engaging in this activity, you have the opportunity to engage in various breathing exercises, aiming to determine the most effective technique for calming your mind. You will enhance your ability to engage in sound reasoning, effectively analyzing and reconciling various aspects of a situation that induces anxiety, thereby enabling the development of effective plans and strategies to address it. The racing mind possesses an inherent inclination to rapidly reach its conclusion. It desires the culmination of events, yet demonstrates indifference towards the occurrences transpiring in the interim. If one is able to acquire the skill of effectively reducing the rapid pace of their thoughts, it can be likened to removing all the ammunition from a firearm's chambers, thereby enhancing one's level of control. You significantly diminish the influence that anxiety exerts over you. Taking deliberate, measured breaths while consciously slowing down cognitive processes and engaging in introspection can be likened to subjecting an ice cube to hot water.

Approaches To Achieving Mastery In Any Field

In the process of honing your skills, you have the opportunity to embody the principle of Kodawari. Please bear in mind that Kodawari is the dedicated pursuit of excellence demonstrated through intentional actions. Therefore, when acquiring a novel skill or enhancing one's inherent abilities, one can employ Kodawari as a means to attain a state of mastery. The essence of Kodawari lies in the pursuit of mastery, emphasizing the process rather than the outcome. It has the potential to propel you towards an ongoing journey of advancement, acquisition of knowledge, and personal development. The following are five strategies to effectively implement Kodawari when endeavoring to acquire expertise or talent:

Don't Fear Discomfort

When embarking upon endeavors that lie beyond the boundaries of your familiar environment, be prepared for the physiological response of shock or panic that may arise within your physical being. Anything that falls beyond the confines of what you perceive as customary will evoke a sense of trepidation and, to a certain degree, pose a potential risk. Given that you have not previously pursued these objectives, you lack a sense of anticipation regarding the potential outcomes. The feeling of discomfort is normal when venturing into the unknown. It serves as an indication that you are displaying an admirable level of bravery and challenging your own boundaries. This is the type of atmosphere crucial for fostering personal growth and self-improvement, therefore, we encourage you to embrace any apprehension, errors, or challenges you may encounter. Do keep in mind that it is not necessary to venture too far beyond the confines of your comfort zone today. Apply slight pressure to the periphery. Gradually, those boundaries will gradually become more pliable and broaden over time.

Exercise prudence in refraining from excessive scrutiny of your plans

While it is commendable to engage in thoughtful planning and deliberate contemplation of one's intended actions, it is crucial to avoid succumbing to the state of analysis paralysis. At a certain juncture in the planning phase, one is prone to excessively analyzing their choices, leading to a state of being overwhelmed and disheartened. Before initiating any action, there are limitations to how much one can foresee. As you strive towards further advancement, you will have the capacity to adapt your strategies in accordance with your circumstances. Masters demonstrate astute foresight and meticulous planning, while simultaneously exhibiting a willingness to embrace calculated risks. They comprehend the notion that deeds carry greater weight than mere words, thus they promptly initiate actions to generate momentum.

This also presents a compelling rationale for embracing a gradual and incremental approach. By proceeding gradually, the level of risk is greatly reduced, thus minimizing the potential disadvantages of immediate action.

Discover the Optimal Position.

In accordance with the writings of Daniel Coyle, notably in his literary work entitled The Talent Code, it is advised that individuals endeavor to achieve a success rate ranging from 60% to 80% during the process of cultivating their skills or talents (The Week Staff, 2015). That is the optimal position where notable enhancements can be achieved. It offers a sufficient level of difficulty to maintain dedication, while also accommodating off days, errors, and unanticipated impediments throughout the journey. When the optimal point of equilibrium is attained, one can effectively sustain their progress over an extended period of time. Your goals possess a suitable level of difficulty, neither excessive nor insubstantial, rendering them suitable for sustained pursuit.

Study a Master

In order to acquire expertise, it is essential to meticulously scrutinize the endeavors of an accomplished individual who has successfully attained the pinnacle of achievement that you aspire to reach in the future. A master can encompass individuals, whether they be family members, acquaintances, or work associates, who are acknowledged as having attained a notable degree of accomplishment within a specific domain. There is no necessity to tackle every challenge in isolation, as there is an abundance of knowledge and wisdom to be gained from individuals possessing the requisite expertise or experience. In this contemporary digital age, the accessibility of renowned experts, distinguished authorities, and influential figures has significantly improved owing to the widespread availability of online platforms such as YouTube, LinkedIn, Instagram, and similar avenues. One can acquire insights into the life of a accomplished individual even without any personal acquaintance by simply observing their videos or paying heed to their podcasts. If you are fortunate enough to have the opportunity to engage with experts face-to-face, make the most of this valuable experience. There is no substitute for engaging in a personal, direct dialogue with a knowledgeable authority and attentively absorbing their insights and guidance concerning your endeavors.

Keep a Notebook

Numerous accomplished artists, entrepreneurs, and inventors maintain journals wherein they can record their concepts, cognitive processes, and encounters. Documenting your thoughts in a journal can effectively alleviate stress levels, enhance cognitive abilities, foster greater self-awareness, and motivate the attainment of personal objectives. In order to enhance your capabilities and aptitudes, it is necessary to maintain a comprehensive documentation of your accomplishments, obstacles, and acquired knowledge, thereby enabling you to make advancements. It will be necessary for you to record and assess both the successes and challenges encountered, identify effective strategies and areas for improvement, and evaluate the psychological ramifications of your experience. Establish a routine of journaling by allocating a small portion of each day to contemplation with a notepad, wherein you can assess your daily advancements and any burdensome thoughts.

Methods For Engaging In Guided Imagery Techniques

We shall utilize the renowned beach setting for this purpose, however, upon experiencing it, envision your very own sanctuary of tranquility. Considering the possibility that the beach may not be the most conducive environment for deep contemplation, I encourage you to explore alternative settings.

- Initially, locate a serene and undisturbed environment
- Take off spectacles or contact lenses and loosen restrictive attire
- Rest in a comfortable position and place your hands on your lap or resting on the arms of your chair
- Next, take some deep and even breaths, directly from your abdomen
- Once a state of relaxation has been achieved, gently shut your eyes and visualize a serene beach with fine, white sand. You are reclining on this shoreline, encompassed by golden grains, gently

swaying coconut palm trees, and pristine azure waves caressing the shore.

The atmosphere is devoid of clouds, allowing the unobstructed rays of the sun to provide a noticeable rise in your body temperature.

- Inhale deeply and savor the fragrance of the tropical flowers and the briny scent of the ocean
- Listen to the rhythmic sounds of the ocean waves crashing and the melodic songs of the birds amidst the surrounding foliage
- Experience the sensation of the warm and inviting sand beneath your skin, and take note of the refreshing taste of a tropical fruit beverage
- Remain in that location for however long is necessary. Observe the considerable increase in tranquility and a heightened state of relaxation within yourself and savor that sensation as it permeates throughout your entire being - starting from the crown of your head, extending to the extremities of your fingers and toes.

"● Observe the significant distance between those sensations of stress and anxiety

When you are prepared, commence a countdown from 10 in reverse order to 1, and gradually unveil your eyes. You shall experience a state of heightened mental awareness accompanied by a profound sense of relaxation.

Meditation

There exists empirical evidence that indicates that the practice of meditation can be effectively utilized to alleviate the manifestations of anxiety and depression, particularly among adult individuals. The practice of mindfulness meditation is experiencing rapid growth as a complementary modality to conventional treatments, including medication, and other adjunctive interventions for social anxiety disorder, such as cognitive behavioral therapy.

When the term "meditation" is brought up, the majority of individuals tend to conjure an image of sitting on the floor, adopting a crossed-legged position, closing their eyes, and engaging in the repetitive chanting of a specific phrase. Although certain meditation practices may incorporate this element, particularly concentrative meditation, mindfulness meditation is characterized by a greater sense of openness and receptivity. We have previously addressed this matter in a prior chapter, albeit in a concise manner. Let us now delve into greater depth and thoroughness in this current section.

History of Mindfulness Meditation

Mindfulness meditation is firmly grounded in the principles of Buddhism, with its origins deeply rooted in the practices of both Zen and Tibetan meditation. It gained initial popularity in the United States following the establishment of the Insight Meditation Society in 1976, a pivotal event catalyzed by the involvement of renowned psychologist Jack Kornfield as one of its co-founders. Subsequently, the prevalence of this undertaking has witnessed a significant surge, bolstered by the contributions of renowned authorities such as John Kabat-Zinn and the establishment of a specialized stress management program. Mindfulness meditation serves as the fundamental element of this program, and has additionally been utilized as a supplementary intervention in conjunction with ACT (Acceptance and Commitment Therapy) since its inception. Furthermore, it has been integrated into various psychotherapy frameworks, such as DBT (dialectical behavior therapy).

What is the objective of practicing mindfulness meditation?

The primary objective of mindfulness meditation is to cultivate a heightened sense of cognitive presence, encompassing both internal and external phenomena. Rather than employing analytic reasoning or emotional responses when confronted with situations or thoughts, you will acquire the skills to detach from your reactions and effectively manage them. As an illustration, in the event that you were on the verge of delivering a speech and detected the onset of tremors in your hands, the practice of mindfulness meditation can effectively assist you in averting feelings of panic, ensuring that they do not escalate into an unmanageable state. You shall have knowledge of the anxious symptom, yet you shall not give it undue attention nor respond to it. Numerous studies have revealed the efficacy of mindfulness meditation in fostering emotional equilibrium, promoting heightened states of relaxation, fostering behavioral regulation, and emancipating individuals from automatic responses.

Two contrasting explanations exist regarding the intended meaning of the term "mindfulness." The initial point is that mindfulness pertains to a cognitive state, while the subsequent point is that it is associated with a specific cognitive process. Both approaches are relevant in this context, as mindfulness can be employed to achieve the desired psychological state, namely, one that is devoid of social anxiety or anxiety in general.

What is the mechanism behind the efficacy of mindfulness meditation techniques?

Mindfulness meditation operates by altering cognitive patterns, focusing abilities, and conscious perception. It cultivates your ability to cultivate mindfulness and engage in detached observation of your emotions and thoughts, without being compelled to react to them. As time progresses, you will gradually become unaccustomed to the extent that you are able to encounter negative emotions and thoughts without eliciting a negative response and without actively seeking comprehension of their nature.

Although negative emotions may evoke discomfort, they are an indispensable facet of existence and hold equal significance for mental well-being as physical pain does for bodily function. Indeed, there exists a medical condition commonly referred to as congenital analgesia, which results in the absence of any tactile or sensory perception of physical pain in affected individuals.

Initially, one might perceive this as a commendable notion, for pain is undoubtedly an abhorrent aspect of human existence. However, it is imperative to deliberate upon this matter more deeply. Discomfort serves as an indicator of underlying issues. For instance, in the event of inadvertently coming into contact with a heated stove, an individual would experience a sensation of pain, thereby signaling the necessity of promptly withdrawing their hand from the source of heat in order to prevent any further harm to their body. Nevertheless, in the event that you are incapable of perceiving such discomfort, persisting to make contact with the stove would inevitably result in significant burn injuries. As a result of this, individuals afflicted with this condition frequently sustain considerably more severe injuries compared to those who accurately perceive pain.

Now, let us consider this in terms of the mind. It is essential that we refrain from seeking elimination of any adverse emotions that may be experienced. Consider fear, for instance. If one finds themselves in an outdoor setting and unexpectedly encounters a wild animal charging towards them, it would be highly advantageous for their personal welfare that they experience the emotive state of fear, subsequently providing them with the impetus to attempt an escape. In the absence of fear, one might persist in their stance, resulting in potential harm or even fatality caused by the animal. Instead of eliminating negative emotions, one must acquire the ability to effectively manage and address them. Anxiety is frequently experienced when there is an excessive reaction to a certain stimulus.

Let us consider this matter from the standpoint of physical suffering once more. Consider a hypothetical scenario wherein every instance of physical contact evokes an intense and agonizing sensation within you. It is implausible that you would be capable of leading a conventional lifestyle given the manner in which you have responded. This holds true when responding to negative emotions with excessive apprehension. Practicing mindfulness can assist in facilitating a healthy response to one's emotions. You shall acquire the ability to sever the link between your anxious thoughts and your excessively anxious panic symptoms and shall proceed to reshape the functioning of your mind.

When incorporated into a therapeutic regimen, mindfulness meditation is focused on addressing targeted issues, such as negative thought patterns or physical manifestations of anxiety. Research findings indicate that engaging in an 8-week course yields significant efficacy in reducing symptoms associated with panic and anxiety. Mindfulness meditation is an effective therapeutic approach for addressing social anxiety disorder, as it has the capacity to positively influence various aspects, including but not limited to attentional processes, cognitive patterns, conscious perception, behavioral tendencies, emotional reactions, spiritual inclinations, and interpersonal bonds.

Throughout the course of therapy, the utilization of mindfulness meditation can serve as a means to enhance one's level of self-awareness regarding the challenges they face. Consequently, this practice aids in modifying one's reactions and responses to said challenges. Typically, it is employed as a means of fostering heightened mindfulness, enhanced self-discipline, and improved capacity to manage emotional responses effectively. In more commonly understood language, mindfulness can be described as a term used to denote self-discipline.

The subsequent mindfulness meditation script can be employed to assist in overcoming social anxiety disorder. The screenplay has been developed using fundamental contemplative techniques, with a specific focus on individuals afflicted with anxiety.

● Locate a serene environment devoid of any disruptions, ensuring to select a designated time during which solitude can be guaranteed.

- Establish a timer for a duration ranging from 20 to 40 minutes, signifying the conclusion of the meditation session – a customary timeframe for such practice.
- Commence by assuming a comfortable position - settle into a chair with a posture that balances comfort with attentiveness; ensure your spine is upright, your feet are firmly planted on the ground, and position your hands in your lap, relaxed and comfortably placed.
- It is imperative to maintain a balanced posture without exerting excessive effort to sustain your position.
- Take off or loosen any garments that are constricting and close your eyes.

Gradually develop an awareness of the level of stillness in your body.

- Take a moment to release tension in your chest, stomach, and shoulders, and shift your attention towards your breathing. - Allow your chest, stomach, and shoulders to relax while directing your attention to your breath. - Take a calm stance by releasing any tension in your chest, stomach, and shoulders and bring your attention solely to your breathing.

- Inhale deeply, drawing the air in through your nostrils, allowing it to reach your diaphragm, and then exhale it out through your mouth.
- Recite once more, allowing the passage of air
- Observe the sense of tranquility that arises as you exhale
- Once you establish a harmonious respiratory pattern, experience the gradual release of tension and stress from your being.
- As one exhales, take note of any cognitions or emotional experiences present. In the event that your thoughts become unfocused or if you experience concern regarding past or future events, it is within the realm of regularity. Do not allow yourself to become overwhelmed by the thoughts that are occupying your mind. Simply recognize and acknowledge their existence.

- Although certain thoughts may incite distress, strive to observe them impartially without passing judgment.
- Take note of the emotions or ideas present - such as an impending social engagement or a dialogue that you perceive could have been more successful.
- If you happen to become engrossed in a negative emotion or thought, take note of it and redirect your attention back to your breathing.
- Endeavor to abstain from self-criticism
- Take note of the sensation without pursuing it, and above all, refrain from allowing your thoughts to chase after it.
- Acknowledge that it is merely a mental construct, observe it, and subsequently release it.

Imagine yourself reclining on the shoreline, feeling the warmth of the sand beneath you. The gentle breeze provides a refreshing sensation as it wafts over your being, accompanied by the soothing sound of the waves caressing the shore, evoking a serene sensation that induces relaxation within your body.

- Focus your attention on regulating your breath, envision it as the ebb and flow of waves and the gentle rustling of wind.
- Maintain composure as the gusts sweep past and the tides surge forward; allow your thoughts to flow and evolve freely. Breathe
- Presently, it is imperative for you to deliberately conjure a specific scenario that elicits sensations of unease or distress. Envision yourself placed in that circumstance and retain the unsettling thoughts within your consciousness. Take a moment to ease your mind and allow those thoughts to drift away. Do not fight against them, rather let them pass by without resistance. Kindly acknowledge and allow them to gradually dissipate
- It is unrealistic to anticipate the complete eradication of anxiety; therefore, refrain from opposing it; instead, embrace it, allow its presence, receive it with open arms, and subsequently release it.

- Take a 15-second interval to consciously observe the passing time, facilitating the process of fortifying and developing novel neural connections in your brain.

The more frequently those pathways are utilized, the more profound the indentation becomes and consequently, the more seamless the process of filling them with positive thoughts will be.

When you are prepared, refocus your attention onto your breathing.

- Direct your focus towards your physical state and subsequently towards the environment surrounding you.
- Gently open your eyelids and extend your limbs

As evident from our discussion, mindfulness meditation encompasses a multitude of stress-reducing therapies previously mentioned. It encompasses techniques such as guided imagery, muscle relaxation, and diaphragmatic breathing, to mention but a few. On account of this formidable amalgamation, many individuals deem this form of meditation to be highly efficacious. Make an effort to incorporate it into your schedule at least once a week, yet engaging in it on a daily basis will yield even more favorable outcomes. Additionally, please note that this is an action that will require ongoing commitment from you in the foreseeable future. It does not function akin to an antibiotic, where it is administered until the illness is completely eliminated, after which the treatment ceases. No, instead, it is imperative that you incorporate it as an integral part of your daily routine.

Engaging In The Application Of Cognitive Behavioral Therapy.

We will demonstrate effective strategies to overcome mental disorders and enhance interpersonal connections. In recent decades, there has been an observable escalation in the implementation of competency-based, collaborative methodologies aimed at providing assistance to clients. Cognitive Behavioral Therapy (CBT) has transitioned its emphasis from identifying the faults or shortcomings of patients to recognizing their strengths and assets. Additionally, it has shifted its attention from the aspects that are not working to those that are functioning optimally.

An essential preliminary measure in effectively addressing a psychological issue entails acquiring further knowledge about it, commonly known as "psychoeducation." This form of informational acquisition pertaining to the problem provides the reassurance that you are not alone, as others have discovered beneficial approaches to surmount it. It would prove beneficial for you to share information about your situation with your friends and family as well. Certain individuals perceive that attaining a precise comprehension of their concerns can greatly contribute to their journey towards recuperation.

Alleviating Anxiety and Depression

To the discerning individual, it becomes evident that anxiety imposes limitations on one's interpersonal engagements, hinders one's willingness to venture beyond their residence, and needlessly impedes their occupational pursuits. Certain individuals may experience anxiety in the aftermath of noticeable traumatic incidents. Primarily, nevertheless, anxiety would gradually intensify devoid of any means of exerting control over it. You may have discerned symptoms indicative of a mental disorder, or alternatively, a mental health professional such as a psychiatrist or physician may have rendered a diagnosis.

Convictions that Inhibit the Experience of Fear

Without exaggeration, it can be stated that anxiety frequently gives rise to significant discomfort. We would like to underscore that we do not intend to discredit your personal experiences, physical symptoms, or distressing thoughts. However, we would like to suggest that you consider adopting certain attitudes aimed at reducing fear. Regard these anxious emotions as an intimidator attempting to exert its dominance by falsely projecting a larger and more formidable presence. You would be inclined to cease this form of intimidation.

Anxiety encompasses cognitive processes outlined below:

Exaggerating the likelihood of a detrimental occurrence.

Exaggerating the potential consequences of the negative event/threat.

Underestimating your capacity to overcome or cope with the adverse occurrence or danger.

Conquer your anxiety and fears by employing the following cognitive strategies as your effective defenses:

Take into consideration the realistic likelihood of the negative event/threat materializing: "There is a possibility, albeit less probable than anticipated."

Gain a comprehensive understanding of the severity of the adverse occurrence/danger. This strategy can be interpreted as the deliberate avoidance of exaggerated negativity, characterized by perceiving situations as undesirable but not catastrophic, unfavorable but not horrific, challenging but not disastrous, demanding but not tragic.

Acknowledge and recognize your own coping skills exhibited thus far. Embrace a mindset of persevering through hardship: 'While it may be unpleasant, I can withstand it,' 'Although it presents challenges, I can endure it,' 'Despite its difficulty, it remains within my capacity to bear.'

Exposing Yourself

Currently, it is imperative to engage in exposure exercises. Exposure exercises entail the identification and confrontation of one's anxieties and apprehensions. Confronting one's fears in a systematic and strategic approach is the most effective means of overcoming mental disorders. While confronting fear may not be an enjoyable experience, it proves to be highly effective. Acknowledge the profound distress caused by your mental condition. Have you grown weary of experiencing life shrouded in a cloak of apprehension? Do you believe that enduring temporary discomfort during exposure exercises is a valuable trade-off for the long-term benefit of overcoming anxiety? The following compilation is of paramount importance in ensuring the successful implementation of impactful exposures:

Ensure that the exposures are appropriately demanding to prompt discomfort, while avoiding extreme levels of difficulty that would discourage you from persisting with the technique.

Persist in subjecting oneself to formidable circumstances and occurrences on a regular basis, incrementally escalating their level of difficulty with each subsequent encounter. One-time isn't enough. As a general principle, persevere in subjecting yourself to those fears on a regular basis until you have become desensitized or habituated to them.

In order for the exposure sessions to be effective, it is essential to ensure their sufficient duration. Please continue to remain in the given situation or event until your feelings of anxiety have diminished by approximately 50 percent.

Make an effort to prevent or manage elements of your anxiety by monitoring your actions.

Throughout the exposure sessions, make every effort to refrain from engaging in any safety behaviors or actions.

Prompt yourself to recall the mnemonic FEAR within the context of Cognitive Behavioral Therapy. It is a phrase that signifies confronting all challenges head-on and achieving recovery.

Have faith in your ability to endure, accommodate, and manage the unease that arises from anxiety. You do not need to like it, but you'll endure it.

Maintain a comprehensive record of your professional experiences and organize them systematically to effectively monitor and chart your growth and advancement.

Fourteenth Day: Indulge in a Soothing Bath

A therapeutic bath is precisely what medical professionals recommend for alleviating anxiety. Allocate a portion of your schedule to indulge in personal leisure and luxuriate in a warm bath. The water will contribute significantly towards alleviating one's stress. To enhance the effectiveness of your bathing experience, it is advised to incorporate a few drops of lavender oil into your bathwater. Lavender has been scientifically demonstrated to alleviate nervous conditions and anxiety as a result of its therapeutic properties. While you indulge in a therapeutic bath, you will simultaneously alleviate tension in your joints and muscles. Your physique will experience a deep sense of relaxation, leading to a noticeable decrease in levels of anxiety.

As you prepare to retire for the night, consider applying a small amount of the oil onto your pillow for added benefit. This will result in a restful slumber, subsequently reducing susceptibility to stress and anxiety. Throughout the day, it is advisable to apply a few drops of lavender onto a handkerchief and inhale deeply in order to achieve mental relaxation. This will prove advantageous in moments of overwhelming anxious thoughts.

Day 15: Dance

Music has a profound impact on one's emotional state, facilitating a significant enhancement in mood while simultaneously mitigating feelings of anxiety. When coupled with the art of dance, one can be assured of experiencing a wholesome physical exercise and an enhanced release of endorphins. This intervention will effectively alleviate feelings of anxiety. However, caution must be exercised when choosing music. It would be advisable not to opt for music that excessively fixates on the adversities of life. You desire a melodious composition that will uplift your spirits and propel you into a joyful state of movement. Please choose your preferred playlist and prepare yourself with appropriate footwear for dancing. Please remember that the focus does not lie on your dance moves. It involves deriving pleasure from the musical compositions and engaging in physical movement. You will experience an improved state of well-being following the completion of the activity, while also facilitating the burning of calories and bringing you closer to achieving physical fitness.

Day 16: Engage in the Activity of Solving a Puzzle Game

One of the effects of anxiety is to cause individuals to retreat from employing logical reasoning. Your concerns assume a magnified prominence, evoking a perception that the situation is beyond your control, leaving you bereft of any potential for positive intervention. This is not right. One must not allow their thoughts to overpower them. It is imperative to reinstate logical reasoning in order to regain command. An excellent approach to accomplish this would be to engage in a puzzle game.

Puzzle games are crafted to facilitate the utilization of logical reasoning. One must exert focus while engaging with them and strategize several steps in advance in order to effectively unravel the puzzle. When engaged in a puzzle game, one is compelled to harness and subdue their unsettled mind. This serves to effectively cultivate focused attention in your brain. Hence, rather than generating pessimistic scenarios, you will adopt an objective perspective towards situations. You will acquire the ability to discern strengths and weaknesses, and strategize on how to emerge victorious. Instead of responding, you will acquire the ability to act with a specific objective in focus.

You may engage in the exploration of word games or block games. A multitude of complimentary puzzle games can be accessed through the Google Play Store. One can opt to download multiple applications and allocate a brief period of time to engage with them, enabling the cultivation of mental acuity and enhanced concentration abilities.

On the seventeenth day, engage in the viewing of a humorous video.

The utilization of laughter as a means to enhance one's mood has been a practice that spans across centuries. When one observes or perceives something humorous, laughter emerges instinctively, thereby instantaneously brightening one's outlook for the day. In contemporary times, one can readily encounter numerous humorous videos on platforms like YouTube. Individuals create these humorous moments as they possess a comprehension that the world periodically yearns for levity. One may utilize such videos as a means to divert one's thoughts, particularly during periods of emotional distress.

An additional benefit of humorous videos lies in their portrayal of ordinary incidents, imparting the lesson of not taking life excessively seriously. One develops the ability to find amusement in oneself instead of perceiving each mishap as a reflection of personal inadequacy. Hence, in instances where circumstances do not unfold as desired, one can respond with laughter and internalize the experience as an opportunity for improvement, abstaining from needlessly harboring self-criticism.

Day 18: Color

Coloring is not exclusively intended for young children, but also extends to individuals of various age groups. Adults can derive enjoyment from it. Indeed, there exist coloring books that have been specially tailored to cater to the interests of adults. Thus, what is the underlying reason behind the effectiveness of coloring? It serves as a means of diversion from one's thoughts by engaging one's attention and fostering presence in the current moment. Coloring is often associated with inducing a sense of tranquility. It offers beneficial effects to both the brain and the nervous system.

Engaging in the activity of coloring can also be considered a type of meditative practice. When engaged in the act of coloring, one must only focus their attention on accurately applying the appropriate hue. While you focus on that task, it is advisable to eliminate all other distractions from your mind and allow your mental state to relax. It is imperative not to entertain distractions, as they may lead to deviating from the intended course of action. Coloring additionally fosters the anticipation of the image that will emerge upon completion of your coloring endeavor. It provides an enjoyable anticipation, which elicits a soothing impact on the mind. Therefore, do not hesitate to add color.

Strategies for Managing Anxiety in the Workplace

Presented herewith are some valuable insights that have proven beneficial to both myself and colleagues with whom I have engaged in dialogue within the professional setting.

Please make an effort to restrict your consumption of coffee in the morning and throughout the day. This will help prevent excessive restlessness. I believe that the consumption of coffee accelerates the release of adrenaline, leading to heightened levels of anxiety.

It is highly recommended to consume ample amounts of water. I understand any potential concerns regarding increased frequency of bathroom visits that may accompany such intake. Indeed, it is possible that you may need to avail yourself of an additional interval for using the restroom. It is indeed beneficial to alleviate anxiety by engaging in physical activity such as walking. I am aware that over time, the human body adapts to the intake of water, resulting in a decrease in frequency of urination.

Make use of all available opportunities to rest. Please refrain from engaging in any activities that may lead to negative consequences. Kindly avail yourself of brief intermissions during which you may engage in ambulatory activities within the confines of the office environment. If it is feasible for you to embark on a brief stroll in the vicinity of the office premises, particularly in the event that atmospheric conditions are favorable, it would be advantageous. The objective is to rise and engage in physical activity to promote circulation.

It may be advisable to seek assistance. If you experience a sense of being overwhelmed whilst engaged in your professional tasks. I notice that your anxiety is increasingly escalating. It would be advisable to assign responsibilities to other individuals. This will assist in reducing your stress and anxiety.

Please ensure that you engage in your deep breathing exercises. Indeed, it is permissible to engage in this behavior even within public spaces. With sufficient practice, one can acquire the ability to execute the task discreetly, ensuring that it goes unnoticed by others. Even in the event that they do, there is no need for concern. It is essential that you prioritize self-care.

I would like to express my sincere gratitude for taking the time to read my book. The process of writing it was quite arduous, as I continue to confront the ongoing struggle of anxiety within my own life. I must express that subsequent to embarking on the process of writing this book, it proved to be invaluable. I feel compelled to proffer my reflections and personal encounters for your consideration. My overarching objective is to provide assistance to the greatest number of individuals within my capacity. I extend my sincerest blessings and well wishes to each and every one of you. It is my fervent hope and earnest prayer that we may all overcome this tumultuous period of anxiety and reclaim our happiness. I desire to foster a life characterized by utmost productivity, joy, affection, and contentment, one that aligns with the true purpose of our existence instead of enduring hardship. I am genuinely convinced that by adhering to my guidance outlined in my book, you can discover an optimal approach to navigating this path in your life. I assure you that by exhibiting resilience and maintaining self-assurance, you will experience improvement and regain a sense of normalcy. Thanks again!!

How To Handle Fear

pharmaceutical

the utilization of glucocorticoids is a pharmacological approach employed to address fear conditioning and phobias by targeting the amygdalae. in a particular study, the disruption of glucocorticoid receptors within the focal cores of the amygdalae was undertaken to enhance comprehension of the mechanisms underlying fear and fear conditioning. lentiviral vectors containing cre-recombinase were employed in mice to impede the glucocorticoid receptors. the findings evidenced that disruption of the glucocorticoid receptors precluded the manifestation of domesticated fear responses. the mice were subjected to auditory cues that elicited a typical freezing response. however, a reduction in freezing behavior was observed in the mice exhibiting suppressed glucocorticoid receptors.

psychology

cognitive behavioral therapy has proven to be efficacious in facilitating individuals' triumph over their phobias. due to the intricate nature of fear, which surpasses mere disregard or elimination of memories, an operational and efficacious approach entails individuals confronting their fears on multiple occasions. by effectively confronting and managing their fearful emotions in a controlled manner, an individual can suppress the recollection or triggering of fear-inducing memories or stimuli.

exposure therapy has been shown to effectively reduce fear in approximately 90% of individuals suffering from specific phobias.

another psychological intervention is systematic desensitization, a form of behavioral therapy employed to completely eradicate the phobia or induce an aversive response to supplant it. the ensuing substitution will be gradual and will occur via a process of conditioning. by virtue of the administration of therapeutic medications, there will be a reduction in muscle tension, and the utilization of specialized breathing techniques will facilitate the alleviation of tension.

worry

anxiety refers to the cognitive, imaginal, affective, and behavioral manifestations of a negative nature in an excessive, uncontrolled manner that arises from a preemptive cognitive risk assessment undertaken to prevent or comprehend anticipated potential hazards and their potential ramifications.

from a psychological standpoint, it can be stated that worry is a form of perseverative cognition, which encompasses the act of persistently contemplating negative events either prior to or in anticipation of the future. worry, in its essence, is an emotional response triggered by genuine or perceived apprehension regarding an array of concerns, often pertaining to one's personal troubles; it embodies a distinct reaction to anticipated future challenges. an excessive level of concern serves as a fundamental indicative factor of generalized anxiety disorder. the majority of individuals encounter occasional episodes of stress in their lives, which are usually of short duration and do not lead to any serious consequences. in fact, a moderate level of stress can have beneficial effects, as it motivates individuals to take precautionary measures (such as fastening their seatbelt or purchasing insurance) or avoid risky behaviors (such as provoking dangerous animals or excessive alcohol consumption). however, individuals who experience excessive worry tend to overestimate potential future risks and unnecessarily magnify the situation, which ultimately leads to a state of stress.

How To Transition From Avoiding Individuals To Embracing Their Participation In Our Personal Development

Earlier in this book, it was elucidated that effective communication possesses the capacity to serve as an adept tool enabling individuals to navigate through various real-life scenarios. This frequently entails acquiring various forms of communication in accordance with the individuals with whom you are engaging in conversation. As an example, the manner in which one engages in communication with their employer in a professional setting is distinguishable from the manner in which one engages in communication with their significant other in a personal context. Within the confines of this document, we shall endeavor to explore diverse modes of communication employed, contingent upon the target audience, as well as demonstrate how proficient utilization of communication aptitude can facilitate adept maneuvering through various scenarios encountered in actuality.

Communication is a skill. This is due to the fact that effective communication is a skill that requires education and dedication, and may not be attainable by all individuals. Abilities are competences that individuals possess and execute proficiently with a notable level of proficiency. This typically does not occur innately and is a skill that can be acquired by individuals.

Communication is among such attributes, and possessing the competence of "effective communication" signifies that one is capable of proficiently exchanging information, both in conveying and comprehending it, with precision and efficiency. This correspondence encompasses matters related to one's emotions, observations, and intangible elements such as concepts and ideas. This is closely related to emotional intelligence and will be elaborated upon in a subsequent section.

Effective Communication within the Corporate Environment

Effective workplace communication entails engaging in professional discourse with individuals whom you maintain professional associations with. A professional association distinguishes itself significantly from intimate relationships such as friendships and familial connections. A formal professional relationship is a continuous exchange between two individuals that adheres to a prescribed set of boundaries considered suitable within the context of their governing standards. The capacity to forge professional connections serves as the foundation for an individual's professional growth and advancement.

Professional relationships encompass a myriad of diverse forms. One relationship that individuals often consider is the association they have with their supervisor or employer, which is perceived as the most prevalent. Alternatively, if you occupy the role of a manager or supervisor, the professional connections you foster are those that you establish with your subordinates. Conversely, professional relationships encompass a multitude of diverse categories beyond those mentioned. Consider the dynamic between a physician and their patient, an attorney and their client, an educator and their student, a service provider and their customer, and the like. Interpersonal dynamics in professional settings exhibit distinct characteristics compared to those of personal relationships, such as friendships and familial bonds. While there remains a notable degree of amiability in numerous professional relationships, it is uncommon for individuals to regard their physician as a personal acquaintance.

Professional relationships are frequently encountered connections that individuals often face challenges in handling. This is owing to its exceptional characteristics compared to various other forms of relationships. When considering the dynamics of friendships, familial bonds, and romantic partnerships, it becomes evident that a shared characteristic among these three is a certain degree of intimacy. In the context of professional relationships, fostering a sense of intimacy is largely discouraged. Indeed, when two individuals involved in a professional association develop a strong bond, it is possible for their acquaintanceship to transition into a friendship that supersedes the professional nature of their relationship.

Numerous individuals are necessitated to acquire anew their aptitude in communication, specifically tailored for the context of professional interactions. While there exists no singular imperative dictating the manner of communication in professional settings, there does exist a general framework guiding appropriate conduct. Thus, what factors contribute to the significant emphasis placed on professional relationships by individuals? What prompts individuals to enroll in courses or engage in educational literature focused on enhancing their proficiency in fostering effective professional relationships?

The immediate response to this inquiry would be that human beings possess an inherent inclination towards sociability; we possess an innate desire for positive social interactions and companionship that is as strong as our biological needs for sustenance and hydration. It is reasonable to assert that strong interpersonal bonds in the workplace significantly contribute to increased happiness and productivity. Additionally, it is paramount to note that the establishment of positive professional relationships affords individuals a greater degree of autonomy and flexibility.

Instead of expending our time and efforts addressing issues stemming from detrimental relationships, we can instead direct our attention solely towards our tasks and prospects. Establishing and fostering strong professional relationships is pivotal when aspiring to cultivate one's career.

In the event that your boss or manager has reservations about your trustworthiness or exhibits an unfavorable opinion of you, it is improbable that they will contemplate your candidacy for a promotion. In general, individuals seek to collaborate with individuals with whom they maintain amicable relationships.

Day 15

Exercise:

Employing items that possess the ability to be stacked, such as rocks, books, boxes, containers, pillows, and similar objects, assemble them methodically and cautiously until they ultimately topple.

In the event of the stack's collapse, maintain composure and exhibit a cheerful disposition.

Many individuals dedicate their lives to accumulating possessions in pursuit of societal-defined success. Individuals accumulate possessions, cultivate knowledge, foster relationships, obtain degrees, amass wealth, secure employment, acquire material possessions, establish enterprises, and partake in diverse experiences, among other endeavors. They experience heightened levels of stress, engage in conflicts, endure fatigue, engage in competition, suffer illnesses, and experience feelings of anxiety and depression as a result of the accumulation process; however, only a scant portion of individuals have managed to attain contentment. In the realm of societal norms, it is commonly preached that achieving an elevated and influential status will lead to the attainment of success. What a deception. What items are you currently arranging in a vertical manner, or what objects do you find yourself driven to arrange in a similar fashion? How is your anxiety contributing to the maintenance of that stack?

Give permission for the stack to descend. This lesson does not promote complacency; rather, it conveys the idea that genuine, genuine, and satisfying work and action can only occur in the absence of the burdensome pressures and concerns associated with excessive accumulation. When engaging in stacking, one's attention is directed towards the future and the perceived significance of the stack; subsequently necessitating the need to uphold and manage that accumulation of nonsensical elements, thus generating a considerable amount of anxiety and pressure. Direct your attention to the current moment and remain engaged in your present experiences; in the event that the stack collapses, respond with a smile and laughter.

An uninterrupted period of 15 minutes characterized by silence and concentrated inhalation and exhalation. Recite the mantra: "I relinquish control as the pile descends."

(Kindly consider sharing your experience using the hashtag #30DaysStack)

Day 16

Exercise:

Assume a reclined position on the floor (not on a mattress or sofa), ensuring that your spine remains erect and your arms lie parallel to your body. Close your eyes.

Now, envision yourself enclosed within a casket or beneath the surface of the earth. Even if this saddens you, proceed with it nonetheless. Using your powers of visualization, envisage a scenario wherein the capacity to open your eyes indefinitely eludes you, accompanied by an inability to maneuver your physique or engage in vocal communication. Remain in this posture for a duration of 10 minutes, or for as extended a period as you are able.

Should this appear gothic or somber, it is solely a reflection of your acquired understanding of the phenomenon of mortality. There exists an age-old doctrine that posits the path to enlightenment lies in a profound cognizance of mortality. The individual who consistently experiences the acknowledgment of their mortality and confronts this reality directly with a composed mindset and genuine acceptance possesses nothing to risk and is authentically liberated to embrace the current moment. The question does not revolve around the inevitability of your physical demise, but rather centers on whether or not you will embrace life prior to your ultimate cessation.

Would you genuinely experience life to its fullest before the eventual demise of your physical being? The current point in time is the sole occurrence that you will consistently encounter. Instead of fearing a pending death, accept it and be thankful for the present moment; and live in it, without anxiety!

Enhancing Sociability In The Professional Environment

Enhancing one's sociability not only facilitates the enhancement of current interpersonal connections but also facilitates the establishment of new friendships and augmentation of personal charisma. Enhanced interpersonal abilities can additionally contribute to improved job performance. Establishing strong professional connections can be achieved by possessing excellent interpersonal abilities. Individuals in the labor force and proprietors who demonstrate increased sociability will effectively draw others towards them.

"If one seeks to enhance their social aptitude within the corporate environment, the following suggestions are certainly beneficial:

1. Develop Communication Skills

Effective communication is essential for cultivating and strengthening relationships, particularly within the context of business. Employers and staff members should possess the ability to comprehend, attentively engage, and effectively communicate their ideas. In the realm of business, all parties involved should exert diligent effort to actively engage in attentive listening, pose thoughtful inquiries, and maintain clarity, thereby ensuring optimal efficacy in communication.

Improvement of writing proficiency is imperative, particularly considering the prevalence of electronic communications in contemporary times. Any error in the tone of written correspondence has the potential to obscure the intended message that a colleague is attempting to convey. The conveyance of information in an inappropriate manner can have detrimental effects on both the trajectory of a business and one's professional journey. If you lack proficiency in written communication, consider enrolling in a course offered by a nearby educational institution or through an online platform, as it can assist you in enhancing your abilities in this domain.

2. Be Pleasant and Approachable

Display sincere and wholehearted smiles conveying a sense of approachability and receptiveness. This has the potential to allure others and alleviate strained responses. By demonstrating the act of smiling to your colleagues or business associates within the workplace, there is a strong likelihood that they will reciprocate with a smile, thereby cultivating a more agreeable and cordial atmosphere. It is important to recognize that in a professional environment, one of the major hindrances to developing meaningful and effective relationships is the tendency to appear overly serious or resistant to adapt to new circumstances.

3. Practice Empathy

Exhibiting empathy enables one to perceive situations from the vantage point of the individual with whom one is interacting. Expressing empathy and comprehending the emotional, physical, and mental repercussions of a particular situation for someone can foster the establishment of a trusting, cohesive, and amicable professional relationship.

4. Exercise Patience in Communication

It is imperative to consistently allocate sufficient time to articulate one's thoughts effectively. To effectively communicate the information, it is advisable to maintain a composed and tranquil disposition. It is important to understand that adopting a relaxed demeanor may facilitate a greater sense of comfort among others. This should not be interpreted as a reason to disregard the importance of maintaining a sense of urgency or to demonstrate a lack of diligence in one's work. This implies that hasty communication has the potential to result in misinterpretations.

5. Appreciate the Perspectives of Others
Assess the veracity of the viewpoints and stances expressed by individuals. Being receptive entails valuing the perspectives of others and demonstrating a willingness to actively engage in listening to them. Moreover, it is imperative that you duly consider these opinions when engaging in your own tasks. Acknowledge the reality that weaknesses may exist within your own viewpoints, and that these can be fortified through the acceptance of input from others.

The significance of the seven primary human emotions?

Depression entails the necessity to reevaluate one's priorities and cultivate a healthy sense of self-worth. It is advisable to focus on undertaking tasks one at a time, avoiding an excessive burden of responsibilities that may generate stress and a feeling of being inundated.

Anger: In the event of experiencing anger, it typically indicates that one's established principles or standards have been transgressed. In such cases, it is imperative to engage in effective communication with the individual involved, making it known that any resulting distress was unintended if one happens to be the cause.

Challenges: The current approach you are employing is proving ineffective, necessitating a need for reassessment. Resetting your goals and discerning that a lack of success does not equate to failure is crucial. By acknowledging this, you have taken a significant stride towards progress.

Remorse: Direct your attention towards the lesson conveyed, and subsequently provide yourself with the reassurance that this transgression shall never be repeated. NOTE: use the power of now to get you out of this thought pattern in conjunction with these 7 revelations.

Being alone implies the necessity of engaging in conversation with an individual.

Insecurity: stems from a dearth of knowledge, necessitating the acquisition of understanding and the fortification of oneself against adversities perceived by one's consciousness as assaults from the external realm.

Pain: Signifies the need for enhanced communication to effectively articulate the reasons behind unmet needs.

It is crucial for you to grasp the concept that your suffering emanates from your own actions and that your identity is not defined by the thoughts generated by your mind. Perhaps this realization had eluded you in the past, but now you possess the awareness required to modify these cognitive patterns, bolstered by the enlightenment and present-moment awareness at your disposal. For instance, in instances where you encounter self-doubt in your thoughts such as "I am unable to accomplish this," it is imperative to substitute them with constructive affirmations such as "I am capable of completing this task," "I have the ability to overcome this challenge," or "This is a minor obstacle compared to what I have successfully achieved before."

Understanding Anxiety Disorder

It is inherent to human beings to experience occasional feelings of anxiety, irrespective of the cause or circumstance. However, individuals diagnosed with anxiety disorders exhibit a distinctive and heightened level of this emotional state. Anxiety disorder is classified as a severe mental disorder, characterized by its various manifestations that result in profound distress and debilitating consequences for individuals it afflicts. The level of panic exhibited by individuals with Anxiety Disorder when engaging in seemingly mundane activities is equivalent to the intensity of panic experienced by individuals without the disorder in highly challenging situations. This can be comprehended with the same degree of ease as an equivalent and intensified state of alarm, albeit originating from entirely distinct factors and occurring on a contrasting magnitude.

Causes of Anxiety Disorders:

Anxiety Disorders remain within the realm of scientific investigation, and a definitive catalogue of identifiable factors remains elusive. Nevertheless, research has demonstrated that certain manifestations of Anxiety disorder can arise as a result of shifts in the environment and alterations in brain functioning. Several research findings indicate that the neural components responsible for the transmission of emotions within the brain can experience inhibition, potentially giving rise to the manifestation of feelings characterized by fear or anxiety that may ultimately culminate in episodes of panic.

Another substantiated factor contributing to the high incidence of Anxiety Disorders is the hereditary transmission through familial lineage, paralleling the heritability patterns observed in several other medical conditions.

Finally, Anxiety Disorder can arise as a consequence of adverse incidents such as trauma or any highly distressing occurrence.

Which individuals are susceptible to developing anxiety disorders?

Anxiety Disorders have been observed to emerge within the psyche during childhood or adolescence, during a stage where situations may be less comprehended. There exists a marginal disparity wherein a slightly higher proportion of females are afflicted with Anxiety Disorder compared to males, resulting in an estimated tally of 19 million known individuals in the United States grappling with this ailment.

Types of Anxiety Disorder:

Panic disorder refers to a manifestation of heightened anxiety characterized by profuse perspiration, chest pain sensation, and an accelerated, forceful heartbeat. These symptoms may create the perception of experiencing a cardiac event for the individual affected. These attacks manifest abruptly, devoid of any forewarning or discernible cause.

Obsessive compulsive disorder (OCD) – falling under the category of Anxiety disorders, this condition encompasses several subtypes, yet fundamentally denotes the presence of specific compulsions that are adhered to with such intensity that they could be aptly described as obsessions. The predominant and familiar manifestation of Obsessive-Compulsive Disorder (OCD) is often characterized by an aversion to germs, although it may also encompass obsessions and compulsions pertaining to numbers, words, or subtle variations in movement. Individuals with OCD will not experience a sense of tranquility unless they meticulously adhere to all prescribed rituals and routines.

Post-Traumatic Stress Disorder (PTSD) refers to a psychological condition characterized by the persistent re-experiencing of a distressing event, either through nightmares or intrusive thoughts, which often stem from a deeply traumatic incident and are commonly linked to feelings of fear and anxiety. Post-traumatic stress disorder (PTSD) is most frequently observed in individuals who have served in the military or are former combatants; however, it can also manifest in individuals who have experienced abuse, sexual assault, or other deeply traumatic circumstances.

Social Anxiety Disorder – individuals diagnosed with social anxiety disorder may occasionally be perceived as reticent or reserved in demeanor. The authentic scenario entails that this disorder is derived from an apprehension of being shunned or humiliated in interpersonal interactions or social contexts. Individuals diagnosed with social anxiety disorder display a tendency to actively maintain a significant physical and emotional distance from others, engaging in minimal social interaction and limiting conversations solely to essential matters.

Phobias – the majority of individuals will develop phobias, and if anyone claims otherwise, it is likely due to not having encountered the specific object or situation they fear. Phobias elicit an intensified state of apprehension and can originate from prevalent phobias like acrophobia, claustrophobia, or ophidiophobia, to more unusual ones such as globophobia or coulrophobia.

Generalized Anxiety Disorder - Much like panic attacks, a generalized anxiety disorder can manifest spontaneously, even without a discernible external stimulus.

Group Therapy And The Application Of Act

Group therapy is often more efficacious than one-on-one counseling for a significant number of individuals. Due to their cost-effectiveness, efficiency in terms of time, and versatility in management, group sessions can seamlessly integrate into various professional and personal settings.

ACT interventions have garnered significant acclaim as a communal intervention aimed at fostering mental well-being and promoting mindfulness, emotional regulation, self-awareness, and the enhancement of personal values. The community practices or activities of ACT foster an environment of openness among its members, enabling them to assume accountability for their personal circumstances.

The implementation of collective strategies or exercises in Acceptance and Commitment Therapy (ACT) cultivates an atmosphere that fosters emotional release and provides the necessary assistance. Actively listening to others and gaining perspectives from diverse viewpoints facilitates a comprehensive comprehension of the concerns faced by individuals. It is widely acknowledged among psychologists that individuals demonstrate a higher tendency to adhere to a course of action when they publicly commit to it, as opposed to merely pursuing an individual goal.

A methodical and problem-solving approach

In the customary context of a professional therapeutic environment, where a substantial number of individuals partake in group therapy, there is generally no room for unconstrained methodologies that may present challenges in evaluation.

In order to optimize time efficiency and enhance the likelihood of receiving favorable responses, the majority of group therapy methodologies adhere to a methodical and sequential framework, wherein all inquiries and assignments are preestablished.

The systematic approach employed by Group ACT serves as a compelling rationale for its suitability in addressing significant variations within populations across diverse cultural and contextual backgrounds.

Greater Recognition

Experiential activities, such as engaging in situational role-playing or participating in directed visualization exercises, serve to deepen individuals' comprehension of alternative perspectives and responses to identical situations. The facilitation of open exchanges fosters an atmosphere of empathy and transparency among the participants.

Several ACT Group Exercises

The Activity Involving Lemons

Take a comfortable seat and prompt the members of the group to contemplate the current situation. If it pleases you, kindly shut your eyes. Please clarify and elucidate your intended meaning in the context of imagining, as it conveys a sensory perception. Subsequently, kindly inquire from them at a measured pace, allowing ample time for contemplation of a porcelain dish and subsequent visualization of a portion of lemon. What do they see? Contemplate the notion of bringing it in close proximity to the olfactory organ. Could you provide a description of the lemon's appearance, please? What does it smell like? Now, should they be prepared, envision undertaking a bite. What is the flavor profile, and allow it to gradually dissipate. Gradually make your way back to the location in which you are currently seated.

For each participant, analyze the exercise to determine the sensory modalities with which they correlated. Contemplate your existing knowledge and disregard any information that eludes your perception. Select the bodily sensations experienced in the absence of the stimulus, and consider the intensity of the sensation. Elucidate that this is merely an uncomplicated innocuous illustration, yet an exceptionally compelling one that showcases the susceptibility of our minds. Let us now delve into the aspects that could potentially result in adverse consequences.

3x3 Exercise

Kindly request the members of the group to close their eyes, provided they are at ease doing so. Otherwise, instruct them to focus their gaze on a fixed point. Therefore, direct one's focus on the breath and prompt individuals to unwind for a brief interval. Kindly elucidate that you intend to request them to momentarily suspend their thoughts and conscientiously reflect upon the current situation. This option would be equally ideal in the event that they choose not to, but please be aware of this.

Kindly request them to reflect on a specific aspect of their physique with which they are dissatisfied, ensuring a moment of uninterrupted contemplation lasting approximately 30 seconds.

Subsequently, inquire of them, allotting an additional interval of 30 seconds for contemplation, to identify something they strongly dislike about an individual in their personal sphere. Lastly, kindly encourage individuals to contemplate on a matter they would prefer to keep concealed from the rest of the group, allocating an additional duration of 30 seconds. Subsequently, proceed to reenter the room with gradual deliberation.

Evaluate, with a focus on the observed thoughts rather than the substance. Establish a connection between this current task and the preceding activity involving Lemon.

Encourage every member of the group to identify the thoughts with which they are most intrigued or willing to collaborate, stemming from the preceding exercise.

Why don't you proceed by recording the concept of the hooked thought on the board, using the symbol T?

I am considering the idea of contemplating T.

I am increasingly contemplating or experiencing the notion that T

Initially, go through the three steps by vocalizing your own thoughts. Subsequently, kindly request every client to perform the same action in a state of complete silence, while attentively observing and acknowledging the ensuing outcome. Prior to proceeding, facilitate the exercise in order to give them the opportunity to repeat if necessary.

Engaging in a Cognitive Contemplation through Singing

Inquire of the individuals within the group whether they are able to identify a melody or harmonic arrangement that corresponds to a perturbing notion. Highlight the possibility that the melody could be perceived as unrefined or foolish, akin to a nursery rhyme or commercial jingle. Providing illustrations and offering personal renditions, if desired, would be highly advantageous. Once the participants have comprehended the exercise, grant the group a suitable period to discover their own melodies, subsequently directing them to raise their fingers upon completion. Please proceed with the exercise and ensure that proper spacing or distancing measures are being maintained. Inform that this procedure is becoming disengaged.

13. Positive Outlook

If one possesses an optimistic outlook, they do not perceive the glass as being half-empty. Rather, you perceive it as being half full. You exhibit the discernment to identify prospects amidst demanding life circumstances. This can be an excellent strategy for combating stress. While both optimists and pessimists encounter similar obstacles in life, empirical research has consistently affirmed that individuals with an optimistic outlook exhibit a superior ability to surmount these challenges compared to their pessimistic counterparts.

According to a sustained research initiative undertaken at the University of Pennsylvania, it has been established that adopting an optimistic mindset possesses favorable implications for one's overall health and well-being. "This approach to life exhibits three overarching traits: "This approach to life showcases three fundamental features: "This approach to life encompasses three primary attributes: "This approach to life demonstrates three key qualities: "This approach to life manifests three principal aspects: "This approach to life embodies three central elements: "This approach to life illustrates three core hallmarks: "This approach to life portrays three essential markers: "This approach to life epitomizes three crucial attributes:

It ascribes any adverse life encounter to specific causes, rather than attributing them to overarching issues. For example, a person with an optimistic outlook would express their condition as follows: "Despite this headache, I am otherwise feeling well."

It attributes various issues to external circumstances instead of internal factors. For example, an optimist would state: 'The inadequate illumination in this room could potentially be the cause of my eye discomfort.' I will endeavor to alter my posture.

It typically presumes that the diverse etiologies of malaise or discomfort tend to be transient or ephemeral. As an illustration, a person with an optimistic outlook will express themselves in the following manner: "Based on my experience, I typically endure cramps for a few hours, thus I am confident in my ability to cope with the existing discomfort."

The positive aspect is that one has the capacity to acquire the skill of thinking optimistically. More precisely, in the event that you experience feelings of anxiety, depression, or a sense of helplessness, it is recommended that you cultivate a positive mindset by engaging in self-dialogue. Could you please explain the process? One method of achieving this objective is by questioning and challenging your negative (pessimistic) thoughts. One can achieve this by challenging each thought by posing inquiries that require evidence for any pessimistic notion that arises in one's mind. For instance, in the event that an individual experiences excessive anxiety prior to a presentation and engages in self-talk that they will be unable to handle the situation or will embarrass themselves, it is advisable to inquire whether there exists any evidence to substantiate such beliefs.

One can proceed to delve deeper into the realm of self-therapy, focusing on the significance and underlying origins of various personal obstacles. An illustration of this would be the following scenario: if you are adhering to a dietary regimen with the aim of shedding pounds, yet find yourself consuming items that you discern as unfit for your goals (such as cake, French fries, and assorted processed foods), there is no need to completely relinquish your efforts and surrender to defeat. On the contrary, it is recommended to reflect upon the duration of your achievements and instances of success in order to cultivate the necessary drive to persist. One can assert, "I must acknowledge my satisfaction with indulging in this cheat meal, but I must also recognize that this shall be my final morsel." I possess the fortitude to persist.

As is evident from the preceding information, the acquisition of optimism through deliberate practical application has the capacity to catalyze a transformative impact on one's life. You simply need to adopt a constructive style of thinking, behavioral planning and self-assessment. Engaging in such behavior can potentially contribute to the advancement of one's physical and mental wellness. And once you reach the point of truly recognizing that your challenges can be effectively addressed and regulated, you will undoubtedly experience a reduction in feelings of apprehension.

Relaxation Techniques

Are you over-worked? When was the most recent occasion in which you experienced restful sleep, unburdened by concerns about the following day's workload? Do you frequently experience the onus of maintaining peak performance? If stress has become an integral part of your daily life, there are numerous methods to cultivate tranquility without incurring the cost of a pricy 90-minute full-body massage.

Truth is, you only need your breath, a pair healthy lungs, and time for yourself that will not take more than 10 minutes.

In this subsequent chapter, we will elucidate a collection of respiration methodologies endorsed by professionals, extensively employed in the realm of meditation, yoga, and various therapeutic modalities.

Essential Information

There is no need to defer attending to your breath until your stress level escalates to the fight-or-flight stage.

Please be advised that practicing controlled breathing techniques facilitates optimal functioning of both the mind and body, assists in maintaining a desirable blood pressure level, fosters relaxation and serenity, and enhances one's ability to combat stress.

Additional research is necessary to fully understand the impact of proper breathing on stress management. However, numerous authorities advocate the utilization of diverse breathing methods to enhance the body's attentiveness and mindfulness, with the aim of attaining the elusive state of Zen.

Actions Required

Wherever you may be situated, be it on your bed, at your desk, or in the living room, these breathing techniques can be employed to help you maintain a sense of serenity even in the presence of overwhelming negativity.

Respiration Equalization (Sama Vritti)

It is always beneficial to achieve a state of equilibrium for your physical well-being.

Take a deep breath and slowly count to four while inhaling, followed by exhaling and counting to four once more. Once you have achieved a state of ease with the balanced breathing technique, you have the option to choose a duration of 6 to 8 counts.

The objectives are to induce a state of tranquility within the nervous system, alleviate stress, and enhance cognitive concentration.

This technique can be practiced at one's convenience and in any location. Nonetheless, according to experts, undertaking this practice shortly before bedtime may yield greater efficacy. This method operates on comparable premises to the act of counting sheep as a means to facilitate sleep. If you are encountering sleep issues, this respiratory strategy can prove advantageous as it aids in pacifying your thoughts and alleviating any interruptions. Consequently, you can allocate your attention towards unwinding your mind and body.

This is perfectly suited for individuals who are in the early stages of acquiring mastery in the application of breathing techniques.

Respirating via the Abdominal Region

Position one hand atop your chest, concurrently situating your other hand upon your abdomen. Take in breath through your nostrils, ensuring that your diaphragm expands adequately with sufficient air. Your objective should be to engage in controlled and deliberate breathing, specifically aiming to achieve a rate of 6 to 10 deep and slow breaths per minute, for a minimum duration of 10 minutes each day. This straightforward respiratory technique is capable of promptly reducing elevated blood pressure levels and mitigating certain cardiac conditions. Employing this methodology for a minimum duration of 6 to 8 weeks enhances its efficacy.

In the event that you are on the brink of undertaking a challenging examination or engaging with a significant client, and you experience feelings of anxiety and stress, employing this particular technique can yield remarkable results in alleviating your apprehensions.

Effortless Relaxation Method

In order to mitigate stress and tension encompassing your entire body, intentionally shut your eyes and direct your attention towards attaining a state of relaxation within each individual muscle group, allocating 2 to 3 seconds for each.

Commence by focusing on your feet and toes, proceed to your knees, followed by your thighs, then shift your attention to your glutes. Next, direct your focus to your arms and hands, then proceed to your neck, and conclude by centering your attention on your jaw, ultimately ending with your eyes. Continuously practice slow and deep breathing as you transition from one bodily region to the next.

If you are encountering challenges in maintaining focus, consider practicing mindful breathing by inhaling through your nostrils, subsequently retaining your breath for a count of 5, all the while ensuring that your muscles remain tensed. Exhale using your oral cavity.

This can be done in any location—be it at one's residence, during work hours at the workstation, or even while travelling. Yet, it is important to remember that you must refrain from inducing dizziness in yourself. If the act of withholding your breath for a duration of at least 5 counts causes discomfort, it is recommended to restrict it to a period of 2 to 3 seconds instead. After attaining a certain level of ease in the following days, you may attempt to prolong the duration of your breath-holding.

Nasal Alternate Nostril Breathing (Nadi Shodhana)

This yoga breathing technique facilitates the restoration of tranquility, promotes equilibrium, and harmonizes the hemispheres of the brain, fostering cohesion between the left and right sides.

The practice commences with assuming a contemplative posture. Please use your right thumb to cover your right nostril and proceed to take a deep breath through your left nostril. Upon reaching the zenith of inhalation, proceed to shield your left nostril with your ring finger and initiate exhalation through the right nostril.

Continue to perform the identical sequence by engaging in inhalation through the right nostril, following it with the act of closing the right nostril through the utilization of the right thumb, and ultimately executing exhalation through the left nostril.

According to yoga practitioners, it is not advisable to engage in this activity before going to sleep as it facilitates the release of energy and stimulates wakefulness.

Visualization

You should promptly proceed to your state of contentment. For proper execution of this visualization technique, it is advisable to engage the assistance of a trained professional such as a therapist or a coach. In the event that the availability of such individuals is limited, a viable alternative would be to utilize audio recording, using your own voice as a guide, which can then be played back during the process.

Essentially, the other individual (or prerecorded audio) is intended to assist you in navigating the procedure. They will offer guidance on regulating your breath and directing your attention towards joyful and optimistic visualizations, all the while assisting you in substituting detrimental thoughts.

This instructed methodology facilitates the attainment of mindfulness. It facilitates the attainment of a state of contentment and fulfillment, preventing one's mind from succumbing to detrimental and tension-inducing contemplations.

This practice can be performed in any location where it is safe and comfortable to close your eyes for a period of time and release all distractions. However, it is important to note that this should not be practiced while operating a vehicle.

Skull Illuminating Respiration Technique

Are you interested in adding some positivity to your day? This approach may prove effective.

This method entails commencing with a prolonged and gradual inhalation, subsequently succeeded by a prompt and forceful exhalation originating from the lower abdomen. Once you have become accustomed to the contraction, you may choose to modify it by conducting a single inhalation and exhalation every 2 seconds, amounting to a total of 10 breaths. Respiration should ideally take place exclusively through the nasal passages.

It is most effective to engage in this practice upon awakening or during periods of emotional distress when one seeks to discover solace or positivity. This method will facilitate the warming up of your body, enhance your energy levels, and stimulate brain activity, particularly beneficial during the initial stages of awakening when your cognitive faculties are still gathering.

The presence of stress, disappointments, frustrations, and various other setbacks that you encounter on a daily basis will persist indefinitely; fortunately, your breath will also continue to be a constant in your life.

18. Maintain a journal to document expressions of gratitude

On a daily basis, establish a routine of jotting down the elements that bring you joy. Please provide a list of the things for which you harbor a sense of gratitude. Record them in your personal journal. Joni Emmerling, a wellness coach, asserts that expressing gratitude for one's blessings effectively counteracts negative thoughts and anxieties.

To promptly alleviate stress proves to be a cost-effective solution. You will not incur any expense. A limited quantity of your time, space, and effort is all that is required.

It is a universal desire for all individuals to experience happiness. However, the pursuit of everlasting happiness is consistently arduous. The world is characterized by such a high level of exigency that the task of staying abreast becomes increasingly arduous.

Nonetheless, over the course of recent years, scientific research has continuously revealed the contributing elements to the experience of happiness. Gratitude is regarded as a fundamental factor in fostering happiness. It is possible that you are already aware of the fact that expressing gratitude has a positive impact on our overall well-being, promoting better sleep, reducing stress levels, and fostering a more optimistic outlook.

Robert A. According to Emmons, a psychology professor at UC Davis,

According to clinical trials, the cultivation of gratitude has been shown to produce significant and enduring outcomes in an individual's life.

However, what actions can one undertake to effectively garner its advantages? Emmons' research, as documented in the esteemed Journal of Personality and Social Psychology, indicates that the practice of maintaining a gratitude journal yields an increase in personal happiness.

Following one month of consistent journaling, there was an observed 10 percent augmentation in the participants' subjective happiness levels. This state of happiness is typically encountered by individuals who have achieved a promotion in their professional occupation.

The conclusion was derived from the analysis of two cohorts comprising participants. A particular cohort was given the directive to record their daily engagements. Meanwhile, the other cohort was directed to document a source of daily happiness.

The results indicate that members of the gratitude group exhibited a greater degree of contentment with their lives when compared to those in the control group. They exhibit a greater degree of positivity and fostered stronger interpersonal connections with their peers.

The researchers reached the consensus that "Engaging in the gratitude condition resulted in significant and consistent enhancements in individuals' evaluations of overall well-being."

Considering the aforementioned discoveries, it can be concluded that material advantages are not essential for attaining happiness. The only items required are a writing instrument, a notepad, and a small amount of available time.

Please compose a list consisting of a minimum of three to five items expressing your gratitude for each day, as well as the preceding day. Please do not be concerned about the less favorable experience. Direct your attention to the benefits.

There is no need for you to give it any consideration. Please kindly articulate the initial affirmative thought that permeates your consciousness. The greater efficacy lies in crafting sentences that are concise and straightforward. Make it a habit. During your journey, you will come to realize that the key to attaining happiness lies within the written words upon a sheet of paper.

19. Art Therapy

In the event that one is unable to attain motivation or experiences a sense of listlessness and despondency, it might be worth considering engaging in the pursuit of artistic endeavors. Art therapy is a therapeutic modality that utilizes creative endeavors to enhance emotional well-being.

The British Association of Art Therapists has provided a formal definition of art therapy as "A therapeutic approach based on the utilization of art materials as the primary means of communication within the psychotherapeutic process." It is utilized by accredited Art Therapists who provide their services to individuals of all age groups, namely children, adolescents, adults, and the elderly.

Throughout this procedure, individuals utilize their ingenuity to produce a piece of art. Fortunately, one does not require artistic talent in order to derive advantages from this therapeutic technique.

The primary objective, henceforth, is to provide temporary respite to the burdened intellect, without the pursuit of perfection. Art therapy has proven efficacy in enhancing one's emotional state. An up-to-date study, for example, unveiled that engaging in coloring activities within books exhibited a positive impact on individuals' emotional state.

According to Dr. Girija Kaimal, the principal investigator of the study, it was inferred that engaging in coloring activities may result in a moderate decrease in distress or negativity. However, due to its structured nature, coloring might not provide the same opportunity for additional creative expression, discovery, and exploration as seen in the open studio condition, which is believed to be responsible for the observed positive mood enhancements.

The engagement in artistic expression does not invariably encompass the act of sketching or drawing. It may assume varied manifestations. Music is among them. One possible alternative in a more formal tone could be: "Potential activities encompass the realm of playing musical instruments as well as vocalizing melodic compositions." Art therapy not only enhances emotional well-being but also confers health-related advantages. Indeed, several studies have revealed that this therapeutic approach proved effective in enhancing the well-being of individuals with cancer.

Being diagnosed with cancer is an exceedingly distressing ordeal. The emotional turmoil frequently gives rise to feelings of depression. Art and dance have been found to be efficacious in mitigating emotional distress, including stress, anger, and sadness. While art therapy commonly necessitates professional guidance, it does not preclude independent expression.

Simply put, it is necessary for you to rekindle your fervor. It may be surprising, but deep within you lies a reservoir of creativity.

Reading the Forehead

The analysis of an individual's forehead provides valuable insights into one's capacity to comprehend and perceive another individual. Although the mobility of the forehead is limited, it is capable of various functions, including the formation of wrinkles and the production of sweat, which can provide significant indications. Many individuals commonly overlook this fact, but those individuals who have acquired expertise in the field of gambling understand that their ability to deceive opponents through bluffing is critical to achieving the desired outcome. Consequently, these skilled gamblers diligently strive to conceal any facial expressions that may inadvertently reveal their thoughts, particularly by concealing their foreheads.

Wrinkled

A furrowed forehead typically stems from an action involving the movement of the eyebrows. In general, the presence of furrows on the forehead generally indicates an individual's intention to emphasize or draw attention to their eyebrow movements or expressions. If you see that someone is furrowing their brows and their forehead wrinkles as well, it is like extreme disapproval or an extreme focus.

Sweaty

When one observes perspiration on another person's forehead, there may exist various underlying causes for this physical phenomenon. They might discover that they are engaging in excessive physical activity, leading to perspiration. The temperatures in the region could potentially be excessively high as well. Nevertheless, it is highly probable that if the temperatures are not the cause, it can be attributed to either fear or arousal.

Gently placing one's hand on the forehead

By observing one's action of gently touching their forehead, it can be discerned that they are attempting to alleviate perspiration. This typically indicates their sense of relief, which could stem from the successful completion of a task or the resolution of a problem they anticipated encountering. When an individual touches their forehead, it may potentially indicate the presence of fear, implying that they are engaged in a personal struggle towards overcoming it. Conversely, it may also involve the act of paying homage to someone as a gesture of reverence or gently placing one's hand on the head as a physical representation of contemplation.

The Analysis of Verbal and Non-Verbal Communication through Oral Cues

When it comes to deciphering the movements of the mouth and lips, one can acquire a plethora of valuable information in a straightforward manner. Simply observe the movements of the mouth and lips, and you will promptly discern an array of diverse emotional expressions.

Flattening lips

When one's lips press firmly against each other, it indicates a conscious effort to refrain from speaking, thereby expressing the desire to withhold certain thoughts or words. It is possible that you possess a measure of disapproval, yet are also inclined towards avoiding potential offense to the other party. Alternatively, you might feel compelled to express your thoughts, but are cognizant of the fact that the current circumstances are neither appropriate nor opportune. Regardless, it can present significant challenges if you were to witness this. Operate under the assumption that the other individual does not possess favorable remarks to relay.

Dropping the lips downward

When the lips assume a downturned position, it typically indicates a certain level of unhappiness or dissatisfaction that demands recognition. This is commonly observed through a facial expression characterized by a frown or grimace, which serves as a clear indication of the individual's discontent towards the current situation.

Parting lips

The act of separating one's lips is of utmost significance. Upon witnessing this behavior, it becomes evident that the individual in question is engaging in flirtatious conduct. This holds especially true when one observes individuals engaging in subtle, coquettish eye contact or exhibiting the act of sticking out their tongue. Nevertheless, this could possibly be suggestive of a mere desire to engage in conversation with another individual while anticipating their response.

Puckering lips

When one purses their lips, it is indicative of displaying a degree of uncertainty regarding the ongoing event. You possess a valid justification for holding a differing opinion or harboring discontent towards it.

Pursing lips

The act of compressing one's lips exhibits a nuanced variation in comparison to the act of forming a pucker. Puckering constitutes a motion used for kissing, whereas pursing one's lips entails the action of drawing them inward and closing them. It typically signifies a certain level of tension, necessitating further observation of accompanying nonverbal cues to ascertain its meaning.

Raising lips up

Upon observing an upward curvature of the lips, it is typically indicative of a rationale behind it—and generally, the connotation is favorable. Typically, a smile is observed, although in conjunction with other discernible indicators, it could also imply sentiments of repulsion.

Sucking on lips

When you retract your lips, you draw them inward, concealing their pink hue within the confines of your mouth. This tendency is commonly indicative of contemplation and uncertainty, although it may also signify an attempt to repress certain thoughts or emotions.

Effective Strategies For Anxiety And Panic Management

Definition

Anxiety often arises when the uncertainty surrounding the future of something we hold dear prevails. For example, one might have concerns regarding punctuality for a job interview or the need to make a favorable impression during an initial romantic encounter. It is characteristic for anxiety to fall within the mild to moderate spectrum. A sufficient amount of concern can assist us in directing our attention, boosting our drive, and enhancing our efficient output. Nevertheless, anxiety can prove to be deleterious once it surpasses a specific threshold.

Anxiousness is a typical human sentiment, and it is an experience shared intermittently by all individuals. Everyone has experienced feelings of apprehension and fear at one time or another. The severity of an individual's anxiety can vary from being minimal to being incapacitating. Despite the unpleasant nature of anxiety, a certain level of apprehension can yield advantages. The present situation would not have arisen had our ancestors not expressed concern about their sustenance. The apprehension of an adverse event prompts us to proactively respond.

Regrettably, an excessive amount of concern has the potential to hinder one's daily functioning. When anxiety reaches an excessive level, it is imperative to proactively address the issue. This chapter will delve into the various manifestations of anxiety and explore how cognitive behavioral therapy can potentially mitigate the symptoms you are experiencing.

Cognitive Behavioral Therapy offers a wide array of tactics to effectively manage and mitigate the symptoms of anxiety. Progressive muscle relaxation and meditation are two methodologies that demonstrate the impact on an excessively stimulated nervous system. Furthermore, cognitive techniques can be utilized to address the exaggerated perception of danger that accompanies anxiety. As an example, this could involve challenging the belief that one will be harshly judged by others in a classroom setting, which is characteristic of social anxiety disorder. Ultimately, confronting our fears directly proves to be another efficacious strategy in managing anxiety; through consistent exposure, the perceived threat posed by dreaded circumstances gradually diminishes.

Assessment

The various manifestations of anxiety can encompass, but are not restricted to, the following:

Panic disorder. This disorder manifests when an individual experiences numerous recurring panic attacks. Episodes of anxiety commonly manifest abruptly and endure for a brief duration. Perspiration, tinnitus, tremors, vertigo, queasiness, respiratory distress, sensation of constriction, irregular heartbeat, and digit numbness all constitute indicative manifestations.

Furthermore, there may be the occurrence of perturbing and swiftly occurring thoughts. One may experience a sense of cognitive disarray, nearness to mortality, or a perpetual onslaught. Anxiety-inducing hormones, such as adrenaline, contribute to the initiation of panic attacks. Adrenaline induces activation of the nervous system, resulting in atypical and alarming sensations.

Phobias. Phobias are characterized by a profound or irrational fear towards certain objects, locations, or living beings. A potential catalyst for a panic attack involves encountering the source of one's phobic stimulus directly.

Generalized Anxiety Disorder (GAD). Generalized Anxiety Disorder (GAD) manifests as a psychological condition wherein individuals experience an overwhelming state of distress attributed to an excessive preoccupation with numerous speculative future scenarios. Due to their perpetual state of apprehension, they encounter challenges when it comes to relaxing. As soon as one of their concerns is mitigated, they promptly shift their focus to another.

Social Anxiety Disorder (SAD). Anxiety about interacting with others. Individuals suffering from Social Anxiety Disorder (SAD) may encounter heightened levels of distress or apprehension when confronted with social settings, including attending social gatherings, reporting to their workplace, encountering unfamiliar individuals, or engaging in casual conversation. If you are afflicted with a social anxiety disorder, you may harbor concerns regarding the perception held by others.

Despite their apparent diversity, these disorders share a common root: excessive worry. Individuals who experience or harbor apprehensions about potential manifestations of an anxiety disorder can derive advantages from engaging in the exercises delineated within this chapter. Please be aware that it is not possible for you to identify your mental disorder. It is advisable to seek a professional evaluation from a medical practitioner or psychologist.

Management

Exposure Therapy

Individuals with anxiety can experience notable advantages through the utilization of cognitive restructuring techniques, which encompass the process of questioning and modifying their beliefs related to their anxiety and its underlying factors. The subsequent content entails a concise summary of the subject matter addressed in preceding chapters; however, it is anticipated to function as a commendable primer on the topic.

- The three stages of cognitive restructuring entail the identification of problematic viewpoints, the evaluation of supporting and contradictory evidence for each notion, and the substitution of these perspectives with more constructive alternatives.

- The ability to ask pertinent questions is a critical component of a reasonable approach.

If one desires to examine a hypothesis, it is recommended to inquire oneself with the following interrogatives:

What guidance would I offer to another individual facing this situation?

If I were to detach myself from these negative emotions, how would I perceive this situation?

- How might an individual with a positive emotional state perceive and comprehend the existing circumstances without experiencing feelings of sadness or anxiety?

- Does the available external evidence corroborate the validity of my hypothesis?

In practical application, the utilization of exposure treatment can be deceptively uncomplicated. The concept is comprehensible in theory, however, its implementation will require a certain degree of courage.

Handling Panic Attacks

Individuals from diverse age groups and backgrounds have the potential to encounter panic episodes, which serve as the chief manifestation of panic disorder. The concept of the event taking place has the potential to trigger them. The underlying cause of an issue is not always readily apparent.

Fortunately, acquiring knowledge about the physiological and psychological processes that occur within your body and mind during a panic attack will enhance your ability to effectively manage and address such episodes.

Upon the realization that an attack is occurring, one's mind may enter a state of heightened agitation marked by frantic contemplation and distress. As one's heart rate elevates, apprehensions may arise regarding potential cardiac detonation. Experiencing lightheadedness is a frequently observed response to a sensation of dizziness. The symptoms you are experiencing stem from the body's natural response to fear. The stress response entails a sequential release of hormones and neurotransmitters, such as adrenaline, by the physiological systems. It is not a deliberate action that can be consciously chosen, but rather an innate, involuntary response that has evolved over time.

Medication-Induced Anxiety" "Pharmaceuticals and their Potential to Induce Anxiety" "The Depiction of Anxiety as an Adverse Effect of Medications

In certain instances, the presence of anxiety is not predominantly associated with the disorder itself, but rather associated with the therapeutic interventions employed to address that disorder. This holds particularly true in the case of medications. Anxiety represents the second most prevalent adverse reaction attributed to pharmaceuticals, surpassed solely by depression. I would like to stress that our discussion extends beyond pharmaceutical treatments for psychological disorders. Pharmaceuticals employed in the management of numerous alternative conditions have the potential to elicit increased levels of anxiety as an adverse reaction. Potent medications invariably have a multitude of outcomes.

In the past, I had the opportunity to attend a conference where I had the privilege of listening to a distinguished pharmacologist, ranked among the top professionals in the field globally. The crux of his discourse revolved around the notion that every medication entails diverse ramifications, and how we categorize these ramifications as either therapeutic or incidental hinges upon our vantage point. It would be impractical to anticipate that medication does not exhibit any adverse effects. Each time a prescription is issued, it will be accompanied by a document, often printed in a font size so minuscule that the aid of a magnifying glass may be required to decipher its contents. This document provides information regarding the medication, recommended dosages, and potential adverse effects or drug interactions. The information provided is typically derived from the Physician's Desk Reference (PDR), an extensive compilation enumerating all available medications along with the aforementioned details. If you are encountering heightened levels of anxiety that appear disproportionate to the situation at hand, it would be advisable to examine the medications you are currently prescribed. You may seek that information available on the Internet, alternatively, you could engage in a discussion with your pharmacist or medical practitioner regarding the medications you are currently consuming. In the event that there exists reasonable grounds to infer that your anxiety may be attributed to the medication, it is highly advisable to consult with your physician regarding the potential reduction of dosage, discontinuation of the medication, or exploration of alternative pharmaceutical options, so as to assess whether these measures may alleviate the symptoms of anxiety.

What is the nature of the experience of secondary anxiety?

At times, when we depict a word as secondary, we inadvertently convey the notion that it carries reduced gravity and potentially may be disregarded. That does not hold true in the context of secondary anxiety. The origin of anxiety holds no significance, as the implications and effects of anxiety remain consistent irrespective of its source. In the subsequent section, we shall address the tangible challenges associated with secondary anxiety and the consequential influence it exerts on individuals' livelihoods.

For the Individual

From the perspective of the individual experiencing anxiety, the distinction between secondary and primary anxiety holds little significance. There may be a modest impact associated with the awareness of anxiety as an adverse reaction to the medications one is consuming, albeit this impact is negligible to the extent that it remains imperceptible. Individuals will continue to experience anxiety, thereby potentially impairing their ability to perform in accordance with their desired level of functionality.

The inclusion of heightened apprehension to an already incapacitating state of depression further hinders an individual's daily functioning. In the context of depression, individuals often encounter challenges in sustaining their focus for a sufficient duration to successfully accomplish tasks. Incorporating unease only serves to introduce an additional diversion and hinder the attainment of optimal performance. The apprehension that an individual undergoes when confronted with a life-threatening ailment may be considered a typical reaction to such circumstances, but it further complicates their ability to respond in an efficient manner. Furthermore, there exists evidence indicating that the presence of anxiety disrupts the regular physiological reactions to illness, consequently exacerbating the overall prognosis.

Certain individuals have a proclivity to perceive the management of anxiety in scenarios similar to the ones delineated in this chapter as superfluous and potentially irrational. That perspective is fundamentally flawed. Within the pages of this literature, my intention has been to underscore the significance of anxiety. In the majority of instances, anxiety deserves our earnest attention as it serves as a profound compass, prompting us to modify our conduct in order to mitigate potential risks. However, in instances where anxiety is subordinate to another underlying process, it frequently indicates that the anxiety no longer serves as a beneficial indicator prompting adaptive behavior. Alternatively, it may foster conduct that is not aligned with our optimal interests. Being secondary does not equate to weakness or the ease of being overlooked. In the event of an automobile collision, the examination of the car's structural components and body panels can be regarded as the primary assessment, with the evaluation of the paintwork damage being of secondary importance. Although it is essential to address the repair of both the frame and panels, it is also imperative to replace the paint coating. In formal tone: "Distinguishable from secondary anxiety is the dissimilarity that in this analogy, the act of painting the car is undertaken subsequent to addressing all other aspects." With secondary anxiety, we often must treat the anxiety while we take care of everything else.

In Honor of Beloved Family and Friends

The impact of secondary anxiety on individuals dear to us is contingent upon the origin of the anxiety and the circumstances at hand. For instance, in cases where a life-threatening illness is the cause of secondary anxiety, it is highly improbable that the individual afflicted with the illness is the sole person experiencing anxiety related to the condition. In the event that your loved one is afflicted with a severe illness, it is only natural that you would experience a sense of unease, as your concerns would not be of lesser significance. Your heightened state of anxiety is a direct result of the circumstances that you currently face. Our esteemed family members hold great significance in our lives; they are the very essence that imbues meaning into our existence. When their lives are endangered, we experience deep concern for their well-being, and we also experience apprehension for our own welfare, given their significance to us.

Expressing our concerns to a person dear to us, whose well-being could potentially be jeopardized by a medical condition, is an inherent and beneficial action. On occasion, individuals may perceive it necessary to conceal their anxiety and direct their attention solely towards the anxiety and ailment experienced by their beloved. Engaging in such behavior has the potential to undermine the integrity of the entire interpersonal connection one shares with the individual in question. Individuals provide support and communicate their emotions with their cherished ones. By confiding your distress to someone who may be in the throes of a terminal illness, you afford them the chance to persist as the compassionate and understanding individual who can offer solace in times of hardship. This could potentially serve as a highly effective method to briefly divert their attention from their personal distress and the tangible illness they are battling.

When faced with situations wherein anxiety arises as a result of factors such as medication, it is of great importance to exhibit empathy towards the individual's anxiety while concurrently assisting and encouraging them in their endeavor to modify the medication in order to alleviate any unwarranted anxiety. In certain circumstances, it may be necessary to intercede with the physician in order to highlight the issue. Should the situation require it, I would be inclined to lend my support. However, I would be more favorably disposed towards advocating for the individual to address those concerns directly with the doctor. The rationale behind this phenomenon lies in the fact that assuming responsibility for managing one's anxiety, despite the fact that it may not be directly caused by oneself but rather by medication, typically fosters an elevation in the individual's self-worth and perception of autonomy. Typically, unmanageable anxiety significantly burdens our self-image.

The Significance Of Couple Stability And The Motivations Behind Its Pursuit

The optimal course of action in such circumstances would be to maintain a consistent level of engagement with your partner. How do you engage in interpersonal communication with your significant other? What method of communication do you utilize? Continuously discussing matters is possible, but resolving lingering issues becomes challenging unless you exhibit communicative humility by aligning with your partner's perspective. An encouraging aspect is that you will collaboratively engage with your partner to address and surpass any emotional susceptibility related to romantic matters. It necessitates a considerable investment of time, effective verbal and written exchange, as well as adeptness in enhancing the bond between individuals.

Allow me to elucidate strategies for managing emotional insecurities.

Addressing the respective requirements of one another

Each and every individual across the globe possesses a multitude of fundamental requisites.

We are all dedicated to ensuring our ability to alleviate pain and suffering.

We seek a broad spectrum of experiences in life.

We desire a sense of significance.

As a result, establishing meaningful connections with others is of utmost importance. All needs are organized within a hierarchical structure based on their relative importance. It is imperative that you acquaint yourself with the critical requirements of your spouse. Does your interpersonal connection contribute to the satisfaction of your emotional requirements? If this is not the case, what steps can be taken to alter the manner in which your partner is regarded and valued?

Balance the Polarity

In all conventional relationships, there invariably exists a balance between masculine and feminine energies. Energy sources of this nature ought not to be contingent upon gender, rather, the existence of opposing forces is necessary in order to attain a state of harmonious romance.

This particular designation is commonly known as polarity. Have you established an unparalleled connection with your significant other? The expression of both masculine and feminine traits in both partners might elicit feelings of anxiety. Over the course of time, these positions have undergone alterations. What measures can be taken to reinstate harmony and eliminate feelings of uncertainty within a relationship?

Value one another as if you were a newly formed couple.

Newly formed romantic partnerships desire to convene and proactively engage with one another on every available occasion. This initial desire diminishes over time. After becoming more acquainted with one's partner, it appears that the mutual appreciation and admiration between the two individuals diminishes. The monotony of everyday existence often leads one to become complacent, resulting in a diminished effort to satisfy one's spouse. The emergence of insecurities becomes evident when your partner perceives a decline in your affection towards them. During this period, it is crucial to rekindle your affection and conduct yourselves as you did during the initial stages of your relationship. Prioritize your spouse above your friends. Express gratitude towards your partner by offering compliments and organizing exceptional outings. Exhibit considerate behavior by crafting affectionate written messages for them. This minor conduct can contribute to reducing anxiety and engendering feelings of desirability in your partner.

Create New Memories

In any interpersonal bond, it is inevitable that errors will arise; however, it is incumbent upon the two individuals involved to ensure that these errors are not allowed to persist. Additionally, should you have encountered challenges pertaining to financial matters in the past, it is imperative to resolve and leave behind these prior issues if you desire to progress as a unified couple.

Strive to cultivate a shift in your attitude instead of insisting that your partner cease engaging in behaviors that disrupt you. Offer your utmost support to your partner as you collectively commit to forging a beautiful narrative, rather than simply seeking solace from the wounds of the past.

Inherent insecurity can arise within even the most resilient interpersonal connections. One cannot exert direct control over their partner's emotions, but it is essential to make every effort to provide them with assistance and encouragement.

What course of action should I pursue if this diminishes my level of vulnerability? Initially, harboring feelings of jealousy may be perceived as endearing, yet unfortunately, it has the potential to foster a toxic division between romantic companions. A significant number of individuals encounter occasional self-doubt, a phenomenon that is inherently human. However, it has the potential to create a divide between you and your partner with regards to jealousy related to communication, personal insecurities, and differences.

To some extent, vulnerability can be advantageous as it fosters emotional closeness within a relationship and amplifies the value assigned to one's partner. However, an excessive amount of fear has the potential to generate a detrimental atmosphere, thereby impairing your self-assurance. Insecurity has the potential to create a rift between partners who share deep affection and concern for each other.

When uncertainty or feelings of envy initially manifest, they often appear harmless and somewhat endearing. Nevertheless, it can compel individuals to exhibit a lack of restraint within a relationship that otherwise appears to be harmonious. To enhance the quality of your relationship, it is advisable for both you and your partner to set forth resolutions. Presented below are several illustrative instances upon which you and your partner should direct your attention.

Self-Esteem

Eliminating self-esteem can be a challenging endeavor, as it is intertwined with one's negative mentality, rendering its eradication a formidable task. Enhancing one's self-esteem serves as the most effective approach to eradicate, or at the very least minimize, one's insecurities. May I inquire as to the method by which you are able to accomplish that task? Boost your morale by scheduling a rejuvenating spa day, commencing a fitness regimen, or engaging in an activity of personal interest. It is optimal to direct your attention towards a challenge that you desire to overcome and subsequently develop strategies to address it.

Determine the Underlying Cause

One cannot disregard any obstacle until one acknowledges its existence. Delve into your thoughts and reflect upon the nature of your current relationship to ascertain the underlying causes of your distress. Did your mother say anything that remained ingrained in your memory from the time you were five years old? Is your significant other engaged in activities that pose an obstacle to your motivation? Regardless, if you have identified the origin of your fear, you are prepared to confront it.

Have confidence in yourself and place trust in your partner.

It is widely acknowledged that confidence plays a pivotal role in fostering contentment and well-being within relationships. The concept of "trust" encompasses more than just the act of confiding in one's spouse with intimate information. It is equally imperative to repose faith in one's instincts. If there has never been a cause for you to harbor skepticism towards your spouse, abstain from doing so! However, should you perceive any semblance of unease within your thoughts, place reliance upon your instincts!

Stop Overthinking

Do not perceive it as a matter of personal concern when your partner makes the decision to spend an evening socializing with their friends, excluding your presence. The actions of your partner are not necessarily intended to cause you harm in any manner. Engaging in sleep before one's partner does not necessarily indicate infidelity; rather, it may simply signify fatigue.

Allowing for Personal Space is Essential to Foster a Sustainable and Flourishing Relationship

It will aid in preventing your partner from experiencing suffocation or being singled out. Additionally, it is imperative to pursue your passions and make a conscious effort to maintain a fulfilling personal life. Engaging in independent tasks will enhance your self-assurance. Please be aware that in addition to your romantic relationships, you still have your individual life to lead.

Release the Grievances of the Past

Previous interpersonal experiences may adversely impact your romantic relationships. It is advisable to cease dwelling on the emotions that an enigmatic former partner had elicited, as doing so may introduce feelings of insecurity into your current relationship. You will only make progress if you release your negative memories.

It would be constructive to engage in conversations with a licensed therapist, trusted individuals in your social circle, close family members, or your present marital partner, regarding your previous encounters. Often, the act of self-expression can yield a therapeutic effect by allowing you to unburden yourself from lingering emotional distress. By openly discussing the painful experiences you have endured in the past, your new life partner will gain a deeper comprehension of your journey. And, to be honest, at times it can be therapeutic to release our emotions.

Don't Stop Conversation

Conversation plays a pivotal role in interpersonal communication and is a frequent topic of discussion in relationship advice resources.

Be Careful

Exercise caution regarding the allocation of your time in social media, as numerous distractions abound within this platform in contemporary times. Certain individuals publicly display their nudity on social platforms, which can lead to a comparison between their physical appearance and that of one's partner, consequently evoking negative sentiments towards their partner's physique. All individuals participating in social media platforms solely share meticulously curated photographs and moments of exceptional quality.

Furthermore, engaging in the act of harassing your partner's former acquaintances on social media will prove futile in addressing and resolving your feelings of insecurity.

www.ingramcontent.com/pod-product-compliance
Lightning Source LLC
Chambersburg PA
CBHW050247120526
44590CB00016B/2253